11/90

Charles Schulz
Great Cartoonist

Marilyn Mascola

illustrated by Luciano Lazzarino

Rourke Enterprises Vero Beach, Florida

Manufactured in the United States of America

Library of Congress Cataloging-in-Publication Data

Mascola, Marilyn, 1949-
    Charles Schulz, great cartoonist / Marilyn Mascola.
      p. cm. —(Reaching your goal)
    Summary: A brief biography of the famous cartoonist who
created the comic strip, "Peanuts." Presents suggestions for
the reader in pursuing a goal.
      1. Schulz, Charles M.—Juvenile literature. 2.
Cartoonists—United States—Biography—Juvenile
literature. [1. Schulz, Charles M. 2. Cartoonists.]
I. Title. II. Series.
PN6727.S3M37 1989
741.5′092′4—dc19
[B]   88-16963
[92]   CIP
ISBN 0-86592-429-5   AC

Do you know Charlie Brown? He's the bald-headed kid in the comic strip *Peanuts*. In 1922, a baby boy was born to Carl and Dena Schulz in St. Paul, Minnesota. The boy looked a lot like Charlie Brown. His name was Charles Monroe Schulz, but everyone called him Sparky.

Sparky grew up to be a famous cartoonist. He is the creator of Charlie Brown and the *Peanuts* gang.

When Sparky was in elementary school, he did very well in all his subjects. He was skipped ahead two grades.

His best subject was art. Sparky loved to draw. His teachers thought Sparky was very talented.

Sparky didn't like being the youngest in his class. He didn't like being the smallest, either. The kids in Sparky's class ignored him and made fun of him. Poor Sparky played alone at recess. He even ate lunch alone.

Every year, Sparky was always the youngest and the smallest kid in class. As time went on, Sparky couldn't keep up with his schoolwork. His good grades started to fall.

But Sparky was still good in art. He liked to draw and to look at pictures others drew. He especially loved the comic strips in the newspapers.

Each Sunday when the newspapers were delivered to the neighborhood store, Sparky ran all the way there. His favorite comic strips were *Popeye* and *Buck Rogers*. He could hardly wait to see what happened next. Sometimes he wondered if he would ever see his own comic strips in the newspaper.

When Sparky was 13, his family was given a black-and-white dog named Spike. Spike was a mixed breed, part pointer and part hound. Spike was smart and funny.

Even Spike seemed to love the comic strips. Just about the time the newspapers were being delivered to the store, Spike would put his paws on Mr. Schulz's chair. "Woof, woof," he barked. It was as if he were saying, "It's time to go get the paper!"

One summer Sparky and his friends organized their own baseball league. His team practiced hard. They day of the big game finally came. Sparky stood on the pitcher's mound. He wound up and pitched the ball. "Strike one!" called the umpire. Sparky threw the ball again. "Strike two!" And again. "Strike three!" Sparky had pitched a no-hit, no-run game. His team came in first place that year. What a wonderful summer that was!

9

When Sparky was in high school, he brought some of his drawings to the yearbook editor. The editor liked them and decided to use them in the yearbook. Sparky was pleased.

On the last day of school, the yearbooks were passed out. Sparky opened his and looked for his drawings. They weren't there! The editor had not used them after all — there were already enough drawings in the book.

After high school, Sparky was determined to be a cartoonist. He started sending his cartoons to newspapers and magazines. He waited eagerly for letters from the publishers. He hoped one of the letters would say, "We want to publish your cartoons." Instead, they all said, "We're sorry. We're not interested in your drawings."

Sparky was hired by an art school. His job was to correct the students' homework. There he made a good friend named Charlie Brown. One day, Charlie saw Sparky working on a drawing. It was a picture of a funny little boy. Sparky decided to name his cartoon boy after his friend Charlie.

Finally, a St. Paul newspaper agreed to publish Sparky's cartoons. Once a week, it printed *Li'l Folks,* the name Sparky first gave to his comic strip.

Some time later, Sparky asked the newspaper to publish his cartoons every day. Instead, they fired him. Was he surprised!

Sparky was not one to give up. He put his
best cartoons together. He mailed them to
United Feature Syndicate in New York City.
Six weeks passed, and Sparky didn't hear from
them. He wrote another letter. "Did you ever
receive my cartoons?" he wrote. "Were they
lost in the mail?"

This time, Sparky got an answer. The letter
said, "We are very interested in your work.
Can you come to New York to talk about it?"

Sparky did go to New York City. He brought
with him a package of his cartoons. When he
arrived at the office of United Feature, no one
was available to see him. He left his package
with the receptionist and said he would come
back later.

By the time Sparky returned, much had already happened. His package had been opened. The people at United Feature loved his cartoon strip. They decided to put it in eight newspapers across the country. The new cartoon strip was called *Peanuts*.

That was in 1950. *Peanuts* now appears in 1,800 newspapers in the United States and Canada. Children and grown-ups all around the world read it. Sparky still does all the drawings and lettering by himself. He uses pencils, pens, ink, paper, a ruler, and a triangle.

People often ask Sparky where he gets his ideas. "Many of the ideas come out of my own childhood," he answers. Sparky draws Snoopy to look a little like his old dog Spike. The *Peanuts* kids wait in movie lines just like Sparky did. Even Charlie Brown's kites get tangled in trees, just like Sparky's did.

Creating the *Peanuts* comics is hard work. Yet Sparky says, "I enjoy going to work each day." When Sparky isn't at work, he is having fun with his family. Sparky is married and has five children. He lives in California at 1 Snoopy Place near Charlie Brown Boulevard. Sparky likes to jog and play paddle tennis. He also likes to play football, baseball, golf, and ice hockey.

Children aren't the only ones who love Sparky's work. Grown-ups love it, too. Sparky has been given the Reuben Award, presented to outstanding cartoonists.

In 1969, the Apollo 10 astronauts honored Sparky in a special way. They named their command module *Charlie Brown* and their lunar module *Snoopy*.

Sparky, or Charles Monroe Schulz, has reached his goal. He draws characters that people around the world love. His cartoons bring joy and laughter to people of all ages. Even when poor old Charlie Brown loses the kite, the little red-haired girl, *and* the baseball game, he keeps on trying. Charlie Brown inspires readers to keep on trying too.

Reaching Your Goal

What are your goals? Here are some steps to help you reach them.

1. **Decide on your goal.**
   It may be a short-term goal like one of these:
   learning to ride a bike
   getting a good grade on a test
   keeping your room clean
   It may be a long-term goal like one of these:
   learning to read
   learning to play the piano
   becoming a lawyer

2. **Decide if your goal is something you really can do.**
   Do you have the talent you need?
   How can you find out? By trying!
   Will you need special equipment?
   Perhaps you need a piano or ice skates.
   How can you get what you need?
   Ask your teacher or your parents.

3. Decide on the first thing you must do.
Perhaps this will be to take lessons.

4. Decide on the second thing you must do.
Perhaps this will be to practice every day.

5. Start right away.
Stick to your plan until you reach your goal.

6. Keep telling yourself, "I can do it!"

Good Luck! Maybe some day you will become a famous cartoonist like Charles Schulz!

Reaching Your Goal Books

Beverly Cleary She Makes Reading Fun

Bill Cosby Superstar

Jesse Jackson A Rainbow Leader

Ted Kennedy, Jr. A Lifetime of Challenges

Christa McAuliffe Reaching for the Stars

Dale Murphy Baseball's Gentle Giant

Dr. Seuss We Love You

Samantha Smith Young Ambassador

Michael Jordan A Team Player

Steven Spielberg He Makes Great Movies

Charles Schulz Great Cartoonist

Cher Movie Star

Ray Kroc Famous Restaurant Owner

Hans Christian Andersen A Fairy Tale Life

Henry Cisneros A Hard Working Mayor

Jim Henson Creator of the Muppets

Rourke Enterprises, Inc.
P.O. Box 3328
Vero Beach, FL 32964